Welcome

I am so glad you are here! Before we begin this new session, I want to take the time and let you know that YOU have been prayed for! It is not a coincidence you are participating in this online Bible study.

My prayer for you this session is simple: **that you will grow closer to our Lord as you dig into His Word each and every day!** As you develop the discipline of being in God's Word on a daily basis, I pray you will fall in love with Him even more as you spend time reading from the Bible.

Each day before you read the assigned Scripture(s), pray and ask God to help you understand it. Invite Him to speak to you through His Word. Then listen. **It's His job to speak to you and your job to listen and obey.**

Take time to read the verses over and over again. We are told in Proverbs to *search and you will find.*

"Search for it like silver, and hunt for it like hidden treasure. Then you will understand."

We are thrilled to provide many different resources for you as you participate in our online Bible study:

- Galatians Study Journal (print out or purchase online)
- Reading Plan
- Weekly Blog posts (Mondays, Wednesdays, & Fridays)
- Weekly Memory Verses
- Weekly Monday Videos
- Weekly Challenges
- Online community: Facebook, Twitter, Instagram, LoveGodGreatly.com
- Hashtags: #LoveGodGreatly #Galatians

All of us here at *Love God Greatly* can't wait to get started with you and hope to see you at the finish line. **Endure, persevere, press on – and don't give up!** Let's finish well what we are beginning today. We will be here every step of the way, *cheering you on!* **We are in this together.** Fight to rise early, to push back the stress of the day, to sit alone and spend time in God's Word! I can't wait to see what God has in store for us this session!

Journey with us as we learn to **Love God Greatly** with our lives!!!

Table of Contents

Love God Greatly consists of a beautiful community of women who use a variety
of technology platforms to keep each other accountable in God's Word.

We start with a simple Bible reading plan, but it doesn't stop there.

Some gather in homes and churches locally, while others connect online with women
across the globe. Whatever the method, we lovingly lock arms and unite for this purpose…

to Love God Greatly with our lives.

In today's fast-paced technology driven world, it would be easy to study God's Word in an isolated
environment that lacks encouragement or support, but that isn't the intention here at *Love God Greatly.*
God created us to live in community with Him and with those around us.

We need each other, and we live life better together.

Because of this, would you consider reaching out and studying with someone this session?

**All of us have women in our lives who need friendship, accountability, and have the desire to dive
into God's Word on a deeper level.** Rest assured we'll be studying right alongside you - learning with
you, cheering for you, enjoying sweet fellowship, and smiling from ear to ear as we watch God unite
women together - intentionally connecting hearts and minds for His glory.

**It's pretty unreal - this opportunity we have to not only grow closer to God through this study, but
also to each other.**

So here's the challenge: call your mom, your sister, your grandma, the girl across the street or the
college friend across the country. Grab a group of girls from your church or workplace, or meet in a
coffee shop with friends you have always wished you knew better. Utilize the beauty of connecting
online for inspiration and accountability, and take opportunities to meet in person when you can.

Arm in arm and hand in hand, let's do this thing… together.

We're proud of you.

We *really* want you to know that.

We're proud of you for making the commitment to be in God's Word… to be reading it each day and applying it to YOUR life - the beautiful life our Lord has given YOU.

Each session we offer a study journal that goes along with the verses we are reading. This journal is designed to help you interact with God's Word and learn to dig deeper - encouraging you to slow down to *really reflect* on what God is saying to you that day.

At *Love God Greatly*, we use the S.O.A.P. Bible study method. Before we begin, we'd like to take a moment to define this method and share WHY we recommend using it during your quiet time.

Why S.O.A.P. it?

It's one thing to simply read Scripture. But when you interact with it, intentionally slowing down to REALLY reflect on it, suddenly words start popping off the page. The SOAP method allows you to dig deeper into Scripture and see more than if you simply read the verses and then went on your merry way. We encourage you to take the time to S.O.A.P. through our Bible studies and see for yourself how much more you get out of your daily reading. You'll be amazed.

What does S.O.A.P. mean?

S- The S stands for Scripture. Physically write out the verses. You'll be amazed at what God will reveal to you just by taking the time to slow down and write out what you are reading!

O- The O stands for Observation. What do you see in the verses that you're reading? Who is the intended audience? Is there a repetition of words? What words stand out to you?

A- The A stands for Application. This is when God's Word becomes personal. What is God saying to me today? How can I apply what I just read to my own personal life? What changes do I need to make? Is there action that I need to take?

P- And finally, P stands for Prayer. Pray God's Word back to Him. Spend time thanking Him. If He has revealed something to you during this time in His Word, pray about it. If He has revealed some sin that is in your life, confess. And remember, He loves you dearly!

EXAMPLE: Read: Colossians 1:5-8

S- The faith and love that spring from the hope that is stored up for you in heaven and that you have already heard about in the word of truth, the gospel that has come to you. All over the world this gospel is bearing fruit and growing, just as it has been doing among you since the day you heard it and understood God's grace in all its truth. You learned it from Epaphras, our dear fellow servant, who is a faithful minister of Christ on our behalf, and who also told us of your love in the Spirit.

O-
- When you combine faith and love, you get hope.
- We have to remember that our hope is in heaven… it is yet to come.
- The gospel is the Word of Truth.
- The gospel is continually bearing fruit and growing from the first day to the last.
- It just takes one person to change a whole community… Epaphras.

A- God used one man, Epaphras, to change a whole town! I was reminded that we are simply called to tell others about Christ -it's God's job to spread the gospel, to grow it, and have it bear fruit. I felt today's verses were almost directly spoken to LGG… *"all over the world this gospel is bearing fruit and growing, just as it has been doing among you since the day you heard it and understood God's grace in all its truth."* It's so fun when God's Word becomes so alive and encourages us in our current situation! My passionate desire is that all the women involved in this Bible study will understand God's grace and have a thirst for His Word. Moved by this quote from my Bible commentary: *"God's Word is not just for our information, it is for our transformation."*

P- Dear Lord, please help me to be an "Epaphras" - to tell others about You and then leave the results in Your loving hands. Please help me to understand and apply what I have read today to my life personally, thereby becoming more and more like You each and every day. Help me to live a life that bears the fruit of faith and love… anchoring my hope in heaven, not here on earth. Help me to remember that the BEST is yet to come!

———————————

Remember, the most important ingredients in the S.O.A.P. method are YOUR interaction with God's Word and your APPLICATION of His Word to YOUR life.

Blessed is the man whose *"delight is in the law of the Lord, and on his law he meditates day and night. He is like a tree planted by streams of water, which yields its fruit in season and whose leaf does not wither. Whatever he does prospers."* ~ Psalm 1:2-3

Soap Reading Plan

		Read	SOAP
WEEK 1	Monday	Galatians Ch1:1-5	Ch1:4-5
	Tuesday	Galatians Ch1: 6-9	Ch1:6-7
	Wednesday	Galatians Ch1:10	Ch1:10
	Thursday	Galatians Ch1:11-17	Ch1:15-17
	Friday	Galatians Ch1:18-24	Ch1:23-24
	Response Day		
WEEK 2	Monday	Galatians Ch2:1-5	Ch2:4-5
	Tuesday	Galatians Ch2:6-10	Ch2:8, 10
	Wednesday	Galatians Ch2:11-13	Ch2:12-13
	Thursday	Galatians Ch2:14-16	Ch2:15-16
	Friday	Galatians Ch2:17-21	Ch2:19-21
	Response Day		
WEEK 3	Monday	Galatians Ch3:1-5	Ch3:2, 5
	Tuesday	Galatians Ch3:6-9	Ch3:8-9
	Wednesday	Galatians Ch3:10-14	Ch3:11, 14
	Thursday	Galatians Ch3:15-20	Ch3:16 & 18-19
	Friday	Galatians Ch3:21-25	Ch3:24-25
	Response Day		
WEEK 4	Monday	Galatians Ch3: 26-29	Ch3:28-29
	Tuesday	Galatians Ch4:1-7	Ch4:4-7
	Wednesday	Galatians Ch4:8-16	Ch4:8-9, 11
	Thursday	Galatians Ch4:17-20	Ch4:17-19
	Friday	Galatians Ch4:21-31	Ch4:23, 31
	Response Day		
WEEK 5	Monday	Galatians Ch5:1-6	Ch5:1, 6
	Tuesday	Galatians Ch5:7-12	Ch5:9
	Wednesday	Galatians Ch5:13-15	Ch5:13-14
	Thursday	Galatians Ch5:16-21	Ch5:16, 19-21
	Friday	Galatians Ch5:22-25	Ch5:22-25
	Response Day		
WEEK 6	Monday	Galatians Ch6:1	Ch6:1
	Tuesday	Galatians Ch6:2-5	Ch6:4
	Wednesday	Galatians Ch6:6-8	Ch6:7-8
	Thursday	Galatians Ch6:9-10	Ch6:9-10
	Friday	Galatians Ch6:11-18	Ch6:14-15
	Response Day		

Goals

We believe it's important to write out goals for each session. Take some time now and write three goals you would like to focus on this session as we begin to rise each day and dig into God's Word. Make sure and refer back to these goals throughout the next six weeks to help you stay focused. YOU CAN DO IT!!!

My goals for this session are:

1.

2.

3.

Signature:_____

Date:_____

Intro into Galatians

The book of Galatians is an amazing little book that packs a punch. It's a book that brings us face to face with the gospel message. **While many assume "the gospel" is something mainly for non-believers, Paul shows us otherwise.**

As Tim Keller says in his book <u>Galatians For You</u>:

"In this short letter, Paul outlines the bombshell truth that the gospel is the A to Z of the Christian life. It is not only the way to enter the kingdom; it is the way to live as part of the kingdom. It is the way Christ transforms people, churches and communities."

We are going to experience Paul's exhortation to the young Christians in Galatia (also meant for us) telling them that all that is necessary - all they need - is the gospel... the good news. Tim Keller says, *"The gospel - the message that we are more wicked than we ever dared believe, but more loved and accepted in Christ than we ever dared hope- creates a radical new dynamic for personal growth, for obedience, for love."*

And that makes our hearts sing!!! **Galatians summarizes the gospel and what it means to our hearts. This, friends, is life changing.**

As we begin, take a moment to meditate on this verse from the beloved book of Galatians:
"I have been crucified with Christ. It is no longer I who live, but Christ who lives in me. And the life I now live in the flesh I live by faith in the Son of God, who loved me and gave himself for me" (2:20).

Here are a few things you need to know about the book of Galatians:

Author:
Paul the apostle. Paul, you may remember, was a former Pharisee that persecuted Christians before Christ got ahold of his heart.

History:
Paul likely wrote this letter around A.D. 48.

Who it is written to and why:
The Galatians. False teachers were infiltrating the church of Galatia, convincing many of the Galatians of the need for things like circumcision, thus dividing the church. Paul's response to the church is exhorting them to return to the gospel alone.

Week 1 Challenge (Note: You can find this listed in our Monday blog post):

Week 1 Memory Verse:

who gave himself for *our sins to deliver us* from the present evil age, according to the *will of our God* and Father, to whom be *the glory forever and ever.*

GALATIANS 1:4-5

LoveGodGreatly.com

Prayer focus for this week: Your Family

	Praying	Praise
Monday		
Tuesday		
Wednesday		
Thursday		
Friday		

Greeting

1Paul, an apostle—not from men nor through man, but through Jesus Christ and God the Father, who raised him from the dead— 2and all the brothers who are with me,

To the churches of Galatia:

3 Grace to you and peace from God our Father and the Lord Jesus Christ, 4who gave himself for our sins to deliver us from the present evil age, according to the will of our God and Father, 5to whom be the glory forever and ever. Amen.

No Other Gospel

6I am astonished that you are so quickly deserting him who called you in the grace of Christ and are turning to a different gospel— 7not that there is another one, but there are some who trouble you and want to distort the gospel of Christ. 8But even if we or an angel from heaven should preach to you a gospel contrary to the one we preached to you, let him be accursed. 9As we have said before, so now I say again: If anyone is preaching to you a gospel contrary to the one you received, let him be accursed.

10For am I now seeking the approval of man, or of God? Or am I trying to please man? If I were still trying to please man, I would not be a servant of Christ.

Paul Called by God

11For I would have you know, brothers, that the gospel that was preached by me is not man's gospel. 12For I did not receive it from any man, nor was I taught it, but I received it through a revelation of Jesus Christ. 13For you have heard of my former life in Judaism,

how I persecuted the church of God violently and tried to destroy it. 14And I was advancing in Judaism beyond many of my own age among my people, so extremely zealous was I for the traditions of my fathers. 15But when he who had set me apart before I was born, and who called me by his grace,16was pleased to reveal his Son to me, in order that I might preach him among the Gentiles, I did not immediately consult with anyone; 17nor did I go up to Jerusalem to those who were apostles before me, but I went away into Arabia, and returned again to Damascus.

18Then after three years I went up to Jerusalem to visit Cephas and remained with him fifteen days. 19But I saw none of the other apostles except James the Lord's brother. 20(In what I am writing to you, before God, I do not lie!) 21Then I went into the regions of Syria and Cilicia.22And I was still unknown in person to the churches of Judea that are in Christ. 23They only were hearing it said, "He who used to persecute us is now preaching the faith he once tried to destroy." 24And they glorified God because of me.

Monday

Read: Galatians 1:1-5

Soap: Galatians 1:4-5

Scripture— Write out the **Scripture** passage for the day.

Observations— Write down 1 or 2 **observations** from the passage.

Applications - Write down 1-2 **applications** from the passage.

Pray — Write out a prayer over what you learned from today's passage.

-Visit our website today for the corresponding blog post!-

Tuesday

Read: Galatians 1:6-9

Soap: Galatians 1:6-7

Scripture— Write out the **Scripture** passage for the day.

Observations— Write down 1 or 2 **observations** from the passage.

Tuesday

Applications - Write down 1-2 **applications** from the passage.

Pray — Write out a prayer over what you learned from today's passage.

Wednesday

Read: Galatians 1:10

Soap: Galatians 1:10

Scripture— Write out the **Scripture** passage for the day.

Observations— Write down 1 or 2 **observations** from the passage.

Applications - Write down 1-2 **applications** from the passage.

Pray — Write out a prayer over what you learned from today's passage.

-Visit our website today for the corresponding blog post!-

Thursday

Read: Galatians 1:11-17

Soap: Galatians 1:15-17

Scripture — Write out the **Scripture** passage for the day.

Observations — Write down 1 or 2 **observations** from the passage.

Thursday

Applications - Write down 1-2 **applications** from the passage.

Pray — Write out a prayer over what you learned from today's passage.

Friday

Read: Galatians 1:18-24

Soap: Galatians 1:23-24

Scripture — Write out the **Scripture** passage for the day.

Observations — Write down 1 or 2 **observations** from the passage.

Friday

Applications - Write down 1-2 **applications** from the passage.

Pray — Write out a prayer over what you learned from today's passage.

Reflection Questions

-CHAPTER 1-

1. Why is Paul considered an apostle?

2. Paul mentions the "gospel" six times in chapter one. What is the gospel and why is it important to know it?

3. In verses 6-9 the Galatians are accused of following a distorted gospel. What does this mean and how is the gospel distorted today?

4. How does Galatians 1:13-15 address this statement: *"God can't love me because I have sinned too much."*?

5. What does it mean to be called by God?

My Response

-CHAPTER 1-

Week 2 Challenge (Note: You can find this listed in our Monday blog post):

Week 2 Memory Verse:

I have been crucified
with Christ
and I no longer live,
but Christ lives in me.
The life I live in the body,
I live by faith
in the Son of God,
who loved me
and gave himself for me.

GALATIANS 2:20

LoveGodGreatly.com

Prayer focus for this week: Your Country

	Praying	Praise
Monday		
Tuesday		
Wednesday		
Thursday		
Friday		

Paul Accepted by the Apostles

1Then after fourteen years I went up again to Jerusalem with Barnabas, taking Titus along with me. 2I went up because of a revelation and set before them (though privately before those who seemed influential) the gospel that I proclaim among the Gentiles, in order to make sure I was not running or had not run in vain. 3But even Titus, who was with me, was not forced to be circumcised, though he was a Greek. 4Yet because of false brothers secretly brought in—who slipped in to spy out our freedom that we have in Christ Jesus, so that they might bring us into slavery— 5to them we did not yield in submission even for a moment, so that the truth of the gospel might be preserved for you. 6And from those who seemed to be influential (what they were makes no difference to me; God shows no partiality)—those, I say, who seemed influential added nothing to me. 7On the contrary, when they saw that I had been entrusted with the gospel to the uncircumcised, just as Peter had been entrusted with the gospel to the circumcised 8(for he who worked through Peter for his apostolic ministry to the circumcised worked also through me for mine to the Gentiles), 9and when James and Cephas and John, who seemed to be pillars, perceived the grace that was given to me, they gave the right hand of fellowship to Barnabas and me, that we should go to the Gentiles and they to the circumcised.10Only, they asked us to remember the poor, the very thing I was eager to do.

Paul Opposes Peter

11But when Cephas came to Antioch, I opposed him to his face, because he stood condemned. 12For before certain men came from James, he was eating with the Gentiles; but when they came he drew back and separated himself, fearing the circumcision

party. 13And the rest of the Jews acted hypocritically along with him, so that even Barnabas was led astray

by their hypocrisy. 14But when I saw that their conduct was not in step with

the truth of the gospel, I said to Cephas before them all, "If you, though a Jew, live like a Gentile and not

like a Jew, how can you force the Gentiles to live like Jews?"

Justified by Faith

15We ourselves are Jews by birth and not Gentile sinners;16yet we know that a person is not justified by

works of the law but through faith in Jesus Christ, so we also have believed in Christ Jesus, in order to be

justified by faith in Christ and not by works of the law, because by works of the law no one will be justified.

17But if, in our endeavor to be justified in Christ, we too were found to be sinners, is Christ then a

servant of sin? Certainly not! 18For if I rebuild what I tore down, I prove myself to be a transgressor. 19For

through the law I died to the law, so that I might live to God. 20I have been crucified with Christ. It is no

longer I who live, but Christ who lives in me. And the life I now live in the flesh I live by faith in the Son of

God, who loved me and gave himself for me. 21I do not nullify the grace of God, for if righteousness were

through the law, then Christ died for no purpose.

Monday

Read: Galatians 2:1-5

Soap: Galatians 2:4-5

Scripture— Write out the **Scripture** passage for the day.

Observations— Write down 1 or 2 **observations** from the passage.

Applications - Write down 1-2 **applications** from the passage.

Pray — Write out a prayer over what you learned from today's passage.

Tuesday

Read: Galatians 2:6-10

Soap: Galatians 2:8, 10

Scripture — Write out the **Scripture** passage for the day.

Observations — Write down 1 or 2 **observations** from the passage.

Applications - Write down 1-2 **applications** from the passage.

Pray — Write out a prayer over what you learned from today's passage.

Wednesday

Read: Galatians 2:11-13

Soap: Galatians 2:12-13

Scripture— Write out the **Scripture** passage for the day.

Observations— Write down 1 or 2 **observations** from the passage.

Wednesday

Applications - Write down 1-2 **applications** from the passage.

Pray — Write out a prayer over what you learned from today's passage.

-Visit our website today for the corresponding blog post!--

Thursday

Read: Galatians 2:14-16

Soap: Galatians 2:15-16

Scripture— Write out the **Scripture** passage for the day.

Observations— Write down 1 or 2 **observations** from the passage.

Applications - Write down 1-2 **applications** from the passage.

Pray — Write out a prayer over what you learned from today's passage.

Read: Galatians 2:17-21

Soap: Galatians 2:19-21

Scripture— Write out the **Scripture** passage for the day.

Observations— Write down 1 or 2 **observations** from the passage.

Friday

Applications - Write down 1-2 **applications** from the passage.

Pray — Write out a prayer over what you learned from today's passage.

-Visit our website today for the corresponding blog post!--

-CHAPTER 2-

1. What does it mean to preach gospel and law?

2. What does it mean that God shows no partiality (Gal 2:6)?

3. How should the fact that Christ lives in you affect your day (vs. 20)?

4. How are we justified?

5. Explain verse 21 in your own words:

My Response

-CHAPTER 2-

Week 3 Challenge (Note: You can find this listed in our Monday blog post):

Week 3 Memory Verse:

So the law was put in charge
to lead us to Christ
that we might be justified by
faith.

GALATIANS 3:24

LoveGodGreatly.com

Week 3

Prayer focus for this week: Your Friends

	Praying	Praise
Monday		
Tuesday		
Wednesday		
Thursday		
Friday		

By Faith, or by Works of the Law?

1O foolish Galatians! Who has bewitched you? It was before your eyes that Jesus Christ was publicly portrayed as crucified. 2Let me ask you only this: Did you receive the Spirit by works of the law or by hearing with faith? 3Are you so foolish? Having begun by the Spirit, are you now being perfected by the flesh? 4Did you suffer so many things in vain—if indeed it was in vain? 5Does he who supplies the Spirit to you and works miracles among you do so by works of the law, or by hearing with faith— 6just as Abraham "believed God, and it was counted to him as righteousness"?

7Know then that it is those of faith who are the sons of Abraham. 8And the Scripture, foreseeing that God would justify the Gentiles by faith, preached the gospel beforehand to Abraham, saying, "In you shall all the nations be blessed." 9So then, those who are of faith are blessed along with Abraham, the man of faith.

The Righteous Shall Live by Faith

10For all who rely on works of the law are under a curse; for it is written, "Cursed be everyone who does not abide by all things written in the Book of the Law, and do them."11Now it is evident that no one is justified before God by the law, for "The righteous shall live by faith." 12But the law is not of faith, rather "The one who does them shall live by them." 13Christ redeemed us from the curse of the law by becoming a curse for us—for it is written, "Cursed is everyone who is hanged on a tree"— 14so that in Christ Jesus the blessing of Abraham might come to the Gentiles, so that we might receive the promised Spirit through faith.

The Law and the Promise

15 To give a human example, brothers: even with a man-made covenant, no one annuls it or adds to it once it has been ratified. 16Now the promises were made to Abraham and to his offspring. It does not say, "And to off springs," referring to many, but referring to one, "And to your offspring," who is Christ. 17This is what I mean: the law, which came 430 years afterward, does not annul a covenant previously ratified by God, so as to make the promise void. 18For if the inheritance comes by the law, it no longer comes by promise; but God gave it to Abraham by a promise.

19Why then the law? It was added because of transgressions, until the offspring should come to whom the promise had been made, and it was put in place through angels by an intermediary. 20Now an intermediary implies more than one, but God is one.

21Is the law then contrary to the promises of God? Certainly not! For if a law had been given that could give life, then righteousness would indeed be by the law. 22But the Scripture imprisoned everything under sin, so that the promise by faith in Jesus Christ might be given to those who believe.

23Now before faith came, we were held captive under the law, imprisoned until the coming faith would be revealed. 24So then, the law was our guardian until Christ came, in order that we might be justified by faith. 25But now that faith has come, we are no longer under a guardian,

Monday

Read: Galatians 3:1-5

Soap: Galatians 3:2, 5

Scripture— Write out the **Scripture** passage for the day.

Observations— Write down 1 or 2 **observations** from the passage.

Monday

Applications - Write down 1-2 **applications** from the passage.

Pray — Write out a prayer over what you learned from today's passage.

-Visit our website today for the corresponding blog post!-

Read: Galatians 3:6-9

Soap: Galatians 3:8-9

Scripture— Write out the **Scripture** passage for the day.

Observations— Write down 1 or 2 **observations** from the passage.

Tuesday

Applications - Write down 1-2 **applications** from the passage.

Pray — Write out a prayer over what you learned from today's passage.

Wednesday

Read: Galatians 3:10-14

Soap: Galatians 3:11, 14

Scripture— Write out the **Scripture** passage for the day.

Observations— Write down 1 or 2 **observations** from the passage.

Applications - Write down 1-2 **applications** from the passage.

Pray — Write out a prayer over what you learned from today's passage.

-Visit our website today for the corresponding blog post!-

Read: Galatians 3:15-20

Soap: Galatians 3:16 & 18-19

Scripture — Write out the **Scripture** passage for the day.

Observations — Write down 1 or 2 **observations** from the passage.

Thursday

Applications - Write down 1-2 **applications** from the passage.

Pray — Write out a prayer over what you learned from today's passage.

Friday

Read: Galatians 3:21-25

Soap: Galatians 3:24-25

Scripture — Write out the **Scripture** passage for the day.

Observations — Write down 1 or 2 **observations** from the passage.

Friday

Applications - Write down 1-2 **applications** from the passage.

Pray — Write out a prayer over what you learned from today's passage.

-Visit our website today for the corresponding blog post!-

-CHAPTER 3-

1. Paul admonishes the Galatians for being foolish. What is their foolishness?

2. What does it mean to be a son of Abraham and how does one become one?

3. Can we rely on the law for salvation? Why or why not? Use Scripture to support your answer.

4. Why do we need Jesus?

5. Explain verses 23-26 in your own words:

My Response

-CHAPTER 3-

Week 4 Challenge (Note: You can find this listed in our Monday blog post):

Week 4 Memory Verse:

But when the time had fully come,
God sent his son,
born of a woman
born under law,
to redeem those under law,
that we might receive
the full rights of sons.

GALATIANS 4:4 & 5

LoveGodGreatly.com

Prayer focus for this week: Your Church

	Praying	Praise
Monday		
Tuesday		
Wednesday		
Thursday		
Friday		

26for in Christ Jesus you are all sons of God, through faith. 27For as many of you as were baptized into Christ have put on Christ. 28There is neither Jew nor Greek, there is neither slave nor free, there is no male and female, for you are all one in Christ Jesus. 29And if you are Christ's, then you are Abraham's offspring, heirs according to promise.

Sons and Heirs

1I mean that the heir, as long as he is a child, is no different from a slave, though he is the owner of everything, 2but he is under guardians and managers until the date set by his father. 3In the same way we also, when we were children, were enslaved to the elementary principles of the world. 4But when the fullness of time had come, God sent forth his Son, born of woman, born under the law, 5to redeem those who were under the law, so that we might receive adoption as sons. 6And because you are sons, God has sent the Spirit of his Son into our hearts, crying, "Abba! Father!" 7So you are no longer a slave, but a son, and if a son, then an heir through God.

Paul's Concern for the Galatians

8Formerly, when you did not know God, you were enslaved to those that by nature are not gods. 9But now that you have come to know God, or rather to be known by God, how can you turn back again to the weak and worthless elementary principles of the world, whose slaves you want to be once more? 10You observe days and months and seasons and years! 11I am afraid I may have labored over you in vain.

12Brothers, I entreat you, become as I am, for I also have become as you are. You did me no wrong. 13You know it was because of a bodily ailment that I preached the gospel to you at first, 14and though my condition was a trial to you, you did not scorn or despise me, but received me as an angel of God, as Christ Jesus. 15What then has become of your blessedness? For I testify to you that, if possible, you would have gouged out your eyes and given them to me. 16Have I then become your enemy by telling you the truth?

much of you, but for no good purpose. They want to shut you out, that you may make much of them. 18It is always good to be made much of for a good purpose, and not only when I am present with you, 19my little children, for whom I am again in the anguish of childbirth until Christ is formed in you! 20I wish I could be present with you now and change my tone, for I am perplexed about you.

Example of Hagar and Sarah

21Tell me, you who desire to be under the law, do you not listen to the law? 22For it is written that Abraham had two sons, one by a slave woman and one by a free woman. 23But the son of the slave was born according to the flesh, while the son of the free woman was born through promise. 24Now this may be interpreted allegorically: these women are two covenants. One is from Mount Sinai, bearing children for slavery; she is Hagar. 25Now Hagar is Mount Sinai in Arabia; she corresponds to the present Jerusalem, for she is in slavery with her children. 26But the Jerusalem above is free, and she is our mother. 27For it is written,

"Rejoice, O barren one who does not bear;
break forth and cry aloud, you who are not in labor!
For the children of the desolate one will be more
than those of the one who has a husband."

28Now you, brothers, like Isaac, are children of promise. 29But just as at that time he who was born according to the flesh persecuted him who was born according to the Spirit, so also it is now. 30But what does the Scripture say? "Cast out the slave woman and her son, for the son of the slave woman shall not inherit with the son of the free woman." 31So, brothers, we are not children of the slave but of the free woman.

Monday

Read: Galatians 3:26-29

Soap: Galatians 3:28-29

Scripture — Write out the **Scripture** passage for the day.

Observations — Write down 1 or 2 **observations** from the passage.

Monday

Applications - Write down 1-2 **applications** from the passage.

Pray — Write out a prayer over what you learned from today's passage.

-Visit our website today for the corresponding blog post!-

Tuesday

Read: Galatians 4:1-7

Soap: Galatians 4:4-7

Scripture— Write out the **Scripture** passage for the day.

Observations— Write down 1 or 2 **observations** from the passage.

Tuesday

Applications - Write down 1-2 **applications** from the passage.

Pray — Write out a prayer over what you learned from today's passage.

Wednesday

Read: Galatians 4:8-16

Soap: Galatians 4:8-9,11

Scripture — Write out the **Scripture** passage for the day.

Observations — Write down 1 or 2 **observations** from the passage.

Applications - Write down 1-2 **applications** from the passage.

Pray - Write out a prayer over what you learned from today's passage.

-Visit our website today for the corresponding blog post!-

Thursday

Read: Galatians 4:17-20

Soap: Galatians 4:17-19

Scripture— Write out the **Scripture** passage for the day.

Observations— Write down 1 or 2 **observations** from the passage.

Thursday

Applications - Write down 1-2 **applications** from the passage.

Pray — Write out a prayer over what you learned from today's passage.

Friday

Read: Galatians 4:21-31

Soap: Galatians 4:23, 31

Scripture — Write out the **Scripture** passage for the day.

Observations — Write down 1 or 2 **observations** from the passage.

Friday

Applications - Write down 1-2 **applications** from the passage.

Pray — Write out a prayer over what you learned from today's passage.

-CHAPTER 4-

1. What was our relationship with God like before our conversion? What is it like after (vs.4-7)?

2. What is the difference between "knowing God" and being "known by God"? How should this affect our times of trials?

3. How can someone become your enemy by telling them the truth (vs.16)?

4. What does it mean to have "Christ formed in you"? How does this happen?

5. Who do the sons of Abraham (Ishmael and Isaac) represent (vs. 22-31)?

-CHAPTER 4-

Week 5 Challenge (Note: You can find this listed in our Monday blog post):

Week 5 Memory Verse:

The entire law is summed up in a single command: Love your neighbor as yourself.

GALATIANS 5:14

LoveGodGreatly.com

Prayer focus for this week: Missionaries

	Praying	Praise
Monday		
Tuesday		
Wednesday		
Thursday		
Friday		

Christ Has Set Us Free

1For freedom Christ has set us free; stand firm therefore, and do not submit again to a yoke of slavery.

2Look: I, Paul, say to you that if you accept circumcision, Christ will be of no advantage to you. 3I testify again to every man who accepts circumcision that he is obligated to keep the whole law. 4You are severed from Christ, you who would be justified by the law; you have fallen away from grace. 5For through the Spirit, by faith, we ourselves eagerly wait for the hope of righteousness. 6For in Christ Jesus neither circumcision nor uncircumcision counts for anything, but only faith working through love.

7 You were running well. Who hindered you from obeying the truth? 8This persuasion is not from him who calls you. 9A little leaven leavens the whole lump. 10I have confidence in the Lord that you will take no other view, and the one who is troubling you will bear the penalty, whoever he is. 11But if I, brothers, still preach circumcision, why am I still being persecuted? In that case the offense of the cross has been removed. 12I wish those who unsettle you would emasculate themselves!

13For you were called to freedom, brothers. Only do not use your freedom as an opportunity for the flesh, but through love serve one another. 14For the whole law is fulfilled in one word: "You shall love your neighbor as yourself." 15But if you bite and devour one another, watch out that you are not consumed by one another.

Keep in Step with the Spirit

16But I say, walk by the Spirit, and you will not gratify the desires of the flesh. 17For the desires of the flesh are against the Spirit, and the desires of the Spirit are against the flesh, for

these are opposed to each other, to keep you from doing the things you want to do. 18But if you are led by the Spirit, you are not under the law. 19Now the works of the flesh are evident: sexual immorality, impurity, sensuality, 20idolatry, sorcery, enmity, strife, jealousy, fits of anger, rivalries, dissensions, divisions, 21envy, drunkenness, orgies, and things like these. I warn you, as I warned you before, that those who do such things will not inherit the kingdom of God. 22But the fruit of the Spirit is love, joy, peace, patience, kindness, goodness, faithfulness, 23gentleness, self-control; against such things there is no law. 24And those who belong to Christ Jesus have crucified the flesh with its passions and desires.

25If we live by the Spirit, let us also keep in step with the Spirit. 26Let us not become conceited, provoking one another, envying one another.

Read: Galatians 5:1-6

Soap: Galatians 5:1, 6

Scripture— Write out the **Scripture** passage for the day.

Observations— Write down 1 or 2 **observations** from the passage.

Applications - Write down 1-2 **applications** from the passage.

Pray — Write out a prayer over what you learned from today's passage.

Tuesday

Read: Galatians 5:7-12

Soap: Galatians 5:9

Scripture — Write out the **Scripture** passage for the day.

Observations — Write down 1 or 2 **observations** from the passage.

Applications- Write down 1-2 **applications** from the passage.

Pray– Write out a prayer over what you learned from today's passage.

Wednesday

Read: Galatians 5:13-15

Soap: Galatians 5:13-14

Scripture— Write out the **Scripture** passage for the day.

Observations— Write down 1 or 2 **observations** from the passage.

Applications - Write down 1-2 **applications** from the passage.

Pray — Write out a prayer over what you learned from today's passage.

-Visit our website today for the corresponding blog post!-

Thursday

Read: Galatians 5:16-21

Soap: Galatians 5:16, 19-21

Scripture— Write out the **Scripture** passage for the day.

Observations— Write down 1 or 2 **observations** from the passage.

Applications - Write down 1-2 **applications** from the passage.

Pray — Write out a prayer over what you learned from today's passage.

Friday

Read: Galatians 5:22-25

Soap: Galatians 5:22-25

Scripture — Write out the **Scripture** passage for the day.

Observations — Write down 1 or 2 **observations** from the passage.

Friday

Applications - Write down 1-2 **applications** from the passage.

Pray — Write out a prayer over what you learned from today's passage.

-Visit our website today for the corresponding blog post!-

-CHAPTER 5-

1. What have we been set free from (vs.1)?

2. What point is Paul making in verse 6?

3. How does the gospel set us free to love others?

4. How are the Spirit and the flesh at war within us?

5. How do we continue to crucify the flesh?

My Response

-CHAPTER 5-

Week 6 Challenge (Note: You can find this listed in our Monday blog post):

Week 6 Memory Verse:

Let us *not* become *weary* in doing *good*, for at the proper time *we will reap* a harvest if *we do not give up.*

GALATIANS 6:9

LoveGodGreatly.com

Prayer focus for this week: Spend time thanking God for how He is working in your life.

	Praying	Praise
Monday		
Tuesday		
Wednesday		
Thursday		
Friday		

Bear One Another's Burdens

1Brothers, if anyone is caught in any transgression, you who are spiritual should restore him in a spirit of gentleness. Keep watch on yourself, lest you too be tempted. 2Bear one another's burdens, and so fulfill the law of Christ. 3For if anyone thinks he is something, when he is nothing, he deceives himself. 4But let each one test his own work, and then his reason to boast will be in himself alone and not in his neighbor. 5For each will have to bear his own load.

6 Let the one who is taught the word share all good things with the one who teaches. 7Do not be deceived: God is not mocked, for whatever one sows, that will he also reap. 8For the one who sows to his own flesh will from the flesh reap corruption, but the one who sows to the Spirit will from the Spirit reap eternal life. 9And let us not grow weary of doing good, for in due season we will reap, if we do not give up. 10So then, as we have opportunity, let us do good to everyone, and especially to those who are of the household of faith.

Final Warning and Benediction

11See with what large letters I am writing to you with my own hand. 12It is those who want to make a good showing in the flesh who would force you to be circumcised, and only in order that they may not be persecuted for the cross of Christ. 13For even those who are circumcised do not themselves keep the law, but they desire to have you circumcised that they may boast in your flesh. 14But far be it from me to boast except in the cross of our Lord Jesus Christ, by which the world has been crucified to me, and I to the world. 15For neither circumcision counts for anything, nor uncircumcision, but a new creation. 16And as for all who walk by this rule, peace and mercy be upon them, and upon the Israel of God.
17From now on let no one cause me trouble, for I bear on my body the marks of Jesus.
18 The grace of our Lord Jesus Christ be with your spirit, brothers. Amen.

Monday

Read: Galatians 6:1

Soap: Galatians 6:1

Scripture — Write out the **Scripture** passage for the day.

Observations — Write down 1 or 2 **observations** from the passage.

Applications - Write down 1-2 **applications** from the passage.

Pray — Write out a prayer over what you learned from today's passage.

-Visit our website today for the corresponding blog post!-

Tuesday

Read: Galatians 6:2-5

Soap: Galatians 6:4

Scripture— Write out the **Scripture** passage for the day.

Observations— Write down 1 or 2 **observations** from the passage.

Tuesday

Applications - Write down 1-2 **applications** from the passage.

Pray — Write out a prayer over what you learned from today's passage.

Wednesday

Read: Galatians 6:6-8

Soap: Galatians 6:7-8

Scripture— Write out the **Scripture** passage for the day.

Observations— Write down 1 or 2 **observations** from the passage.

Applications - Write down 1-2 **applications** from the passage.

Pray — Write out a prayer over what you learned from today's passage.

-Visit our website today for the corresponding blog post!-

Thursday

Read: Galatians 6:9-10

Soap: Galatians 6:9-10

Scripture— Write out the **Scripture** passage for the day.

Observations— Write down 1 or 2 **observations** from the passage.

Thursday

Applications - Write down 1-2 **applications** from the passage.

Pray — Write out a prayer over what you learned from today's passage.

Read: Galatians 6:11-18

Soap: Galatians 6:14-15

Scripture— Write out the **Scripture** passage for the day.

Observations— Write down 1 or 2 **observations** from the passage.

Applications - Write down 1-2 **applications** from the passage.

Pray — Write out a prayer over what you learned from today's passage.

Reflection Questions

-CHAPTER 6-

1. According to verse 1, are we to point out everyone's sin? Why or why not?

2. How do we mock God?

3. What is our motivation to "not grow weary" (vs 9)?

4. What is the one thing we should brag about and why?

5. Thinking over the whole book, what is Paul most passionate about? Why is he so upset with the Galatians?

My Response

-CHAPTER 6-